The Family of William Cooksey of Cumberland County, Kentucky

*from William Cooksey of Kentucky
to the Illinois generation*

ISBN-13: 978-1978175440
ISBN-10: 1978175442

by M. L. Moeller

a descendant of William Cooksey

The courthouse burned to the ground during a civil war skirmish.

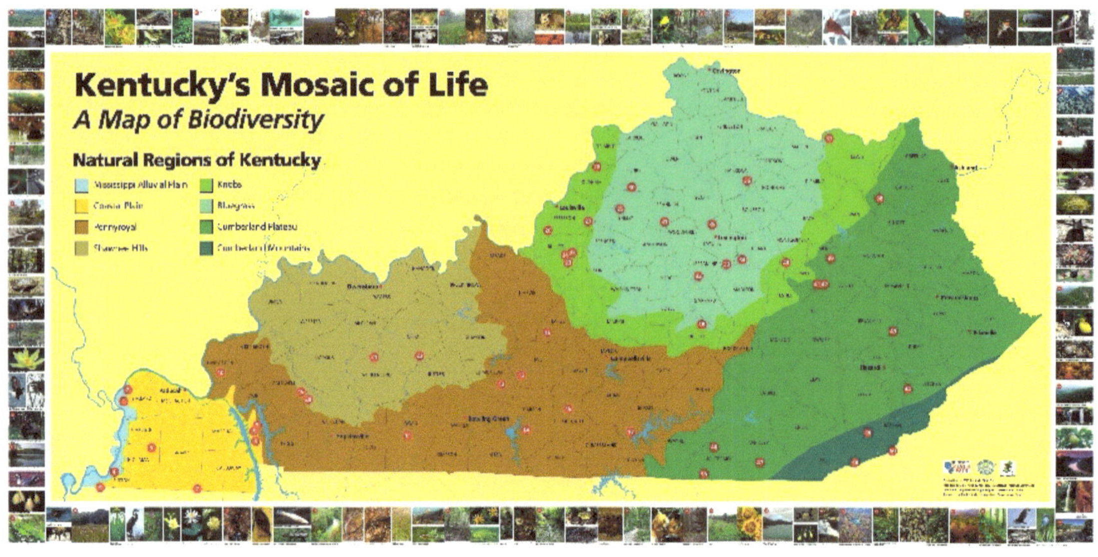

Cumberland county in Kentucky is centered around the Cumberland River. This is an aerial view of the region. Just imagine the hardship for the original settlers who came either, up from Tennessee or over the mountains from the Virginia settlements.

CONTENTS

To Russell who inspires me to be the best at whatever I attempt to do. Thank you for being in my life.

Generation One

1. **William[1] Cooksey**, was born about 1790 in Kentucky.
   He married 'unknown'.

   > *Children:*
   2. i. Samuel[2] Cooksey was born about 1813.

1830 United States Federal Census for William Cooksy
Kentucky › Cumberland › North Of Cumberland River

Name																	
William A Bladroe	1			1									1				
Winny Williams		1	1	1	1								1		1		
William Ray	1	1		1			1						1			1	
William Dubuery				1					1			1					
William Wright	2	1			1					2		1					
Martin Low	1			1					3		1						
William Brown	1			1					3		1						
William Nunn					1						1						
William Huckison	1			2							1						
William Cooksy	2		1		1				1	2		1					
William H Waite	1			1							1						
Walter Nunn		1	3			1			1	1	1			1			
	10	4	1	5	9	3	"	1	1	9	5	1	4	5	2	2	"	1

In the 1830 Census for the Federal Government it lists as William's household these people:
> *Males over 20: 1*
> *Females over 20: 1*
> *Males from 15-19: 1*
> *Females from 5-9: 2*
> *Females under 5: 1*

Total listed for his household was 6. 2 adults and 4 children under 20. Only 1 male is listed as under 18.

2. **Samuel[2] Cooksey** (William[1]), was born about 1813 in Cumberland County, Kentucky, and died about 1855.

    He married Martha Elizabeth Riddle, who was born April 17, 1818 in Burksville, Cumberland County, Kentucky, and died November 2, 1904 in Rivoli, Mercer County, Kentucky.

Martha Elizabeth (Riddle) Cooksey

Martha: Elizabeth Riddle was born at Burkesville, Cumberland county, Kentucky, April 17, 1813, and died in New Windsor November 2, 1904, aged 91 years, 6 months and 16 days. She was married to Samuel Cooksie in the year 1832. To this union were born seven children, five sons and two daughters. Of those living are Mrs. David Young, William, Mrs. Sarah Young, and G. W. of New Windsor and Timothy of Galesburg. James died at the age of fourteen years. Israel died at the age of nine months. She joined the M.E. Church at an early age and after coming to this country she joined the U. B. church and lived a Christian life.

Funeral services were held from the Free Mission church on Thursday at 11 a.m., Rev. George Williams officiating and burial was in the New Windsor cemetery.

The cemetery she is actually listed in is Petrie. I am thinking that about the time she died they incorporated a newer cemetery as the New Windsor cemetery.

> *Children:*
> i. James[3] Cooksey was born about 1834 in Cumberland County, Kentucky.
> ii. Israel Cooksey was born about 1836 in Cumberland County, Kentucky.
> 3. iii. Clarissa C. Cooksey was born March 27, 1837.
> iv. William Albert Cooksey was born about 1839 in Cumberland County, Kentucky, and died February 26, 1927 in Rivoli Township, Mercer County, Illinois.
> 4. v. Sarah Ann Cooksey was born October 24, 1841.
> 5. vi. Timothy F. Cooksey was born April 16, 1843.
> 6. vii. George W. Cooksey was born 1852.

#			Name	Age	Sex	Occupation	
23	148	148	Jacob Brake	63	M	Farmer	30
24			Washington Brake	38	F		
25			S. J. Brake	8	F		
26			M. Brake	5	F		
27			W. N. Brake	4	M		
28			J. B. Brake	2	M		
29			M. E. Brake	16	F		
30	149	149	Samuel Cooksey	37	M	Farmer	9
31			E. Cooksey	35	F		
32			C. N. Cooksey	13	F		
33			W. A. Cooksey	11	M		
34			S. A. Cooksey	9	F		
35			J. F. Cooksey	6	M		
36	150	150	Nathan Riddle	38	M	Farmer	1
37			Lucy Riddle	36	F		
38			F. A. Riddle	14	M		
39			S. A. Riddle	12	F		
40			C. J. Riddle	10	F		
41			J. M. Riddle	7	M		
42							

The 1850 Census for Samuel Cooksey and his family. He died sometime between 1850 and 1860. Either in Kentucky or in Illinois. Various spellings of the Cooksey surname include: Cooksey, Coosie, Cooksie and so on.

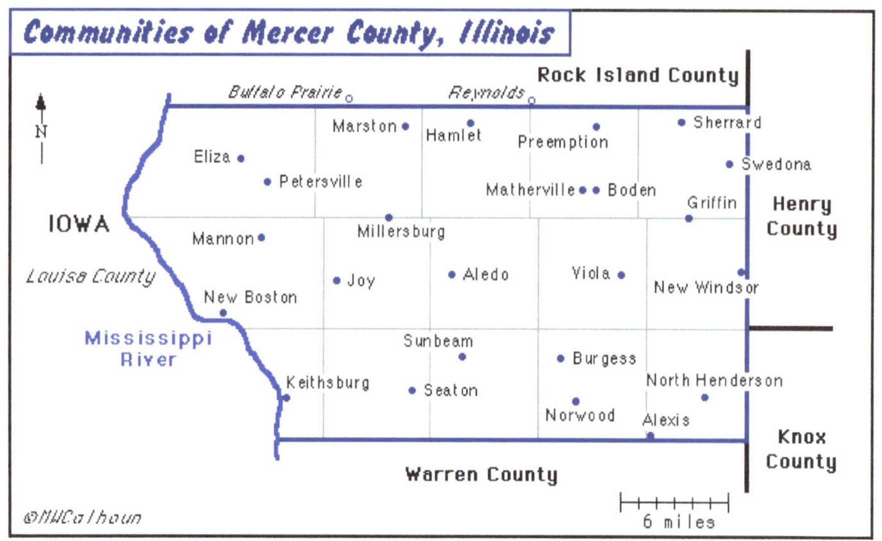

Mercer County, Illinois images

3. **Clarissa C.[3] Cooksey** (Samuel[2], William[1]), was born March 27, 1837 in Cumberland County, Kentucky, and died May 14, 1920 in Mercer County, Illinois. She was buried May 1920 in New Windsor Cemetery, New Windsor, Mercer County, Illinois.[1]

She married (1) George Elliot Potter, April 6, 1857 in Knox County, Illinois. He was born December 16, 1835 in Ohio, and died May 19, 1909 in Missouri. He was buried May 1909 in Isadora Cemetery, Isadora, Worth County, Missouri.[2]

David and Clarissa (Cooksey) Young's headstone

She married (2) David Young, who was born July 4, 1844 in Illinois, and died March 4, 1917 in Monroe County, Illinois. He was buried March 1917 in New Windsor Cemetery, New Windsor, Mercer County, Illinois.

   Children:
   i. Sarah[4] Young was born October 1869 in Mercer County, Illinois, and died September 3, 1870 in Mercer County, Illinois. She was buried September 1870 in New Windsor Cemetery, New Windsor, Mercer County, Illinois.[3]

Sarah Young (born October 1869)

7.   ii.   Blanche A. Young was born about 1873.
         iii. Charles Young b. about 1876 in Mercer County, Illinois.

Charles Young headstone

4. **Sarah Ann³ Cooksey** (Samuel², William¹), was born October 24, 1841 in Cumberland County, Kentucky, and died March 23, 1912 in New Windsor, Mercer County, Illinois. She was buried March 1912 in Hopewell Cemetery, New Windsor, Mercer County, Illinois.

Joseph and Sarah Ann (Cooksey) Young headstone

She married Joseph Young, February 28, 1861 in Knox County, Illinois. He was born February 23, 1833 in Essex County, New York, and died June 28, 1898 in New Windsor, Mercer County, Illinois. He was buried July 1898 in Hopewell Cemetery, New Windsor, Mercer County, Illinois.[4]

    Children:
8.   i. William Frank⁴ Young was born December 10, 1861.
    ii. Elihu Young was born 1864 in New Windsor, Mercer County, Illinois, and died August 15, 1935 in Galesburg, Knox County, Illinois.
    iii. John Young was born 1866 in New Windsor, Mercer County, Illinois, and died December 18, 1934 in Moline, Rock Island County, Illinois.
    iv. Timothy D. Young was born 1868 in Illinois, and died March 30, 1954 in Coal Valley, Henry County, Illinois. He was buried April 1954 in Hopewell Cemetery, New Windsor, Mercer County, Illinois.[5]

Timothy and Elizabeth (Cooper) Young headstone

He married Elizabeth A. Cooper, August 15, 1894 in Knox County, Illinois. She was born May 25, 1858 in Viola, Mercer County, Illinois, and died March 14, 1902 in Viola, Mercer County, Illinois. She was buried March 1902 in Hopewell Cemetery, New Windsor, Mercer County, Illinois.[6]

v. Clara Bell Young was born 1871 in Illinois, and died May 28, 1942 in Kankakee, Kankakee County, Illinois.
She married George Fred Harbour, December 10, 1896 in Mercer County, Illinois.

vi. George Young was born 1871 in New Windsor, Mercer County, Illinois, and died February 24, 1941 in New Windsor, Mercer County, Illinois.

George and Anna Young headstone

vii. Martha J. Young was born January 1, 1874 in New Windsor, Mercer County, Illinois, and died. January 17, 1934 in Alpha, Henry County, Illinois.

5. **Timothy F.[3] Cooksey** (Samuel[2], William[1]), was born April 16, 1843 in Cumberland County, Kentucky, and died October 22, 1919 in Galesburg, Knox County, Illinois. He was buried October 1919 in Henderson Cemetery, Henderson, Knox County, Illinois.

23 Oct 1919
T. F. COOKSEY
T. F. Cooksey died at the Galesburg Hospital yesterday at 5:20 p.m. He had been ill only a week and the cause of his death was a complication of diseases.
The deceased was born April 16, 1848, in Cumberland county, Ky. When a small boy, he came to Illinois with his parents and has made this community his home since that time. He was united in marriage to Margaret Waters, Dec. 19, 1875 and to this union two sons were born. He made his home with his son, Albert, since the death of his wife, two years ago. He was well liked by all who knew him and will not only be missed by his family but also by many friends and near relatives.
Those surviving are two sons, Forrest who resides near Oneida, and Albert of near Henderson; one granddaughter, Margaret, one brother William of New Windsor and several nieces and nephews.

Timothy and Margaret (Waters) Cooksey headstone

He married Margaret Waters, December 30, 1875 in Knox County, Illinois. She was born 1848 in Pennsylvania, and died 1917 in Knox County, Illinois.

> *Children:*
>   i. Horace E.[4] Cooksey was born about 1883 in Illinois.
>   ii. Forrest E. Cooksey was born 1882 in Illinois, and died 1952 in Knox County, Illinois. He was buried 1952 in Henderson Cemetery, Henderson, Knox County, Illinois.

Forrest and Selena (Willets) Cooksey headstone

MRS. SELENA COOKSEY

Mrs. Selena Cooksey, 90, of 335 N. Cedar St., died Sunday at 5:15 p.m. at Cottage Hospital.

The former Selena Willetts was born April 17, 1887, in Chariton, Iowa, and married Forrest Cooksey Feb. 10, 1915, in Rock Island. He died in 1952.

She was a member of the Reorganized Church of Jesus Christ of Latter Day Saints.

Surviving are two brothers, Floyd Willetts, Galesburg, and John Willetts, LaFeria, Tex.

Funeral will be Wednesday at 3 p.m. at Hinchliff - Pearson - West Chapel. Burial will be in Henderson Cemetery, Henderson. No visitation is planned.

Selena Cooksey obituary

> *He married Selena Willetts, February 10, 1915 in Rock Island, Rock Island County, Illinois. He was born April 17, 1887 in Chariton, Iowa, and died December 17, 1977 in Galesburg, Knox County, Illinois. She was buried December 1977 in Henderson Cemetery, Henderson, Knox County, Illinois.[7]*

9.   iii. Albert Cooksey was born December 3, 1885.

6. **George W.[3] Cooksey** (Samuel[2], William[1]), was born 1852 in Kentucky, and died 1917 in Illinois. He was buried 1917 in New Windsor Cemetery, New Windsor, Mercer County, Illinois.[8]

Ida Stonefelt

George W. Cooksey headstone

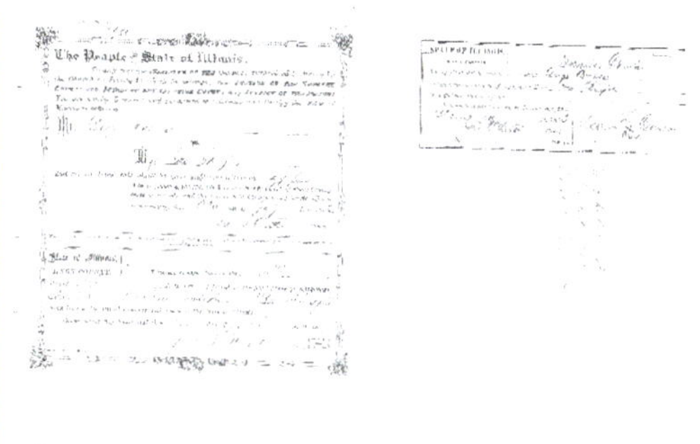

Marriage certificate for Ida and George Cooksey

He married (1) Ida Stonefelt, July 25, 1873 in Knox County, Illinois. She was born about 1851 in Sweden.

> *Children:*
> i.   Sarah[4] Cooksey was born October 16, 1875 in Illinois, and died February 8, 1877 in Mercer County, Illinois.

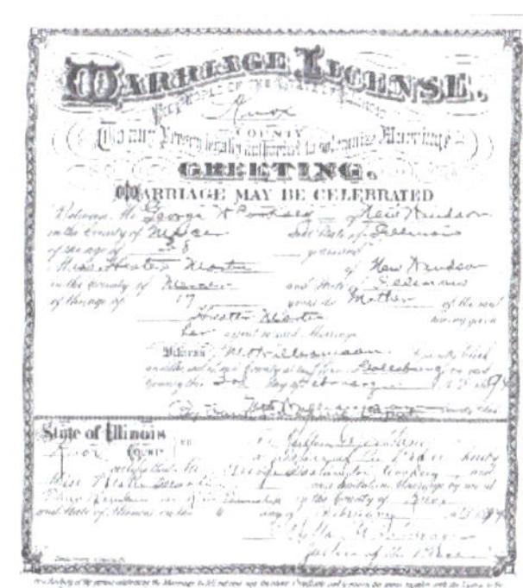

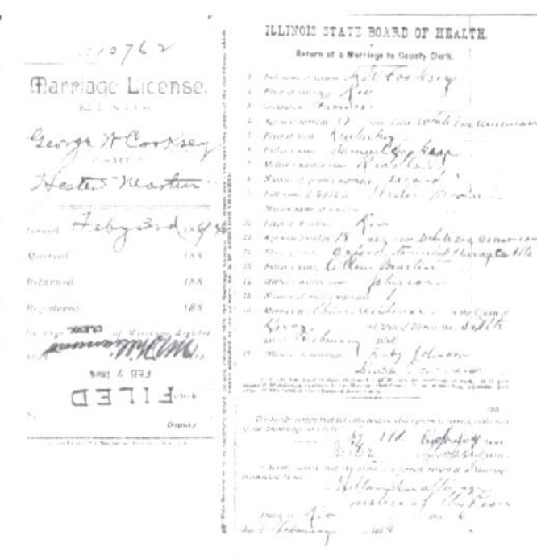

Marriage Certifiate for George and Hester Cooksey

Hester Martin Cooksey

He married (2) Hester "Esther" Martin, February 6, 1894 in Knox County, Illinois.[9] She was born July 1875 in Illinois (daughter of Allen Martin and Mary M. Johnson), and died 1963 in Lynn Township, Knox County, Illinois.

> *Children:*
> ii. James A. Cooksey was born April 18, 1898 in Illinois, and died April 4, 1919 in Knox Township, Knox County, Illinois.[10]

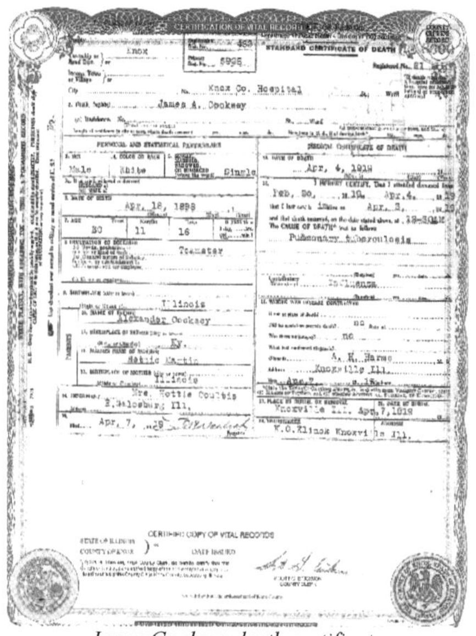

James Cooksey death certificate

     iii. 'unknown' Cooksey was born 1900, and died 1900.

10.   iv. Walter Arthur Cooksey was born April 9, 1901.

11.   v. Georgia Lucille Cooksey was born February 1, 1908.

     vi. Sarah E. Cooksey was born about 1905 in Mercer County, Illinois.

Generation Four

7. **Blanche A.[4] Young** (Clarissa C.[3] Cooksey, Samuel[2], William[1]), was born about 1873 in Mercer County, Illinois.

Edward and Blanche (Young) Norris headstone

She married Edward Norris, February 17, 1892 in Mercer County, Illinois.

> *Children:*
> i. George[5] Norris was born about 1893, and died October 26, 1918. He was buried October 1918 in New Windsor Cemetery, New Windsor, Mercer County, Illinois.

George Norris headstone

> ii. Cromwell H. Norris was born 1893 in Mercer County, Illinois, and died 1975. He was buried 1975 in New Windsor Cemetery, New Windsor, Mercer County, Illinois.[11]

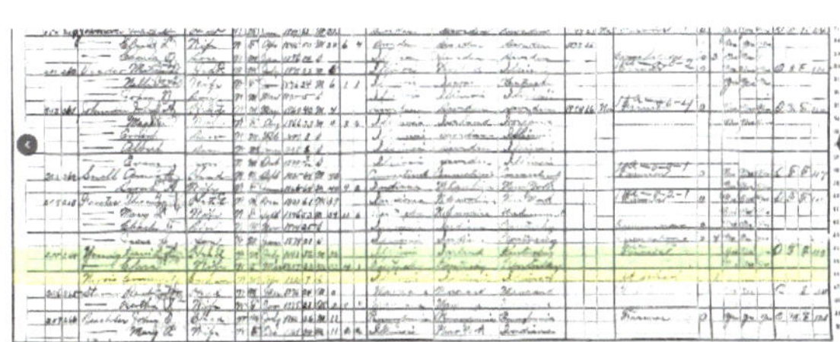

1900 Federal Census for Cromwell Norris. He was living with Grandparents.   *Cromwell Harvey Norris headstone*

ii. Otis Norris was born November 24, 1897 in Mercer County, Illinois, and died December 1981. He was buried December 1981 in New Windsor Cemetery, New Windsor, Mercer County, Illinois.[12]

Otis Norris headstone

8. **William Frank[4] Young** (Sarah Ann[3] Cooksey, Samuel[2], William[1]), was born December 10, 1861 in Mercer County, Illinois, and died August 11, 1942 in Rock Island, Rock Island County, Illinois.
He married Wilhemina Herzberg, May 2, 1899 in Illinois. She was born September 23, 1880 in Cable, Illinois, and died July 3, 1930 in New Windsor, Mercer County, Illinois.

Children:
12. i. Martha Tracy[5] Young was born October 9, 1901.
     ii. Joseph Arthur Young was born July 27, 1903 in New Windsor, Mercer County, Illinois, and died February 26, 1984 in Rock Island, Rock Island County, Illinois.
13. iii. William Horace Young was born December 26, 1905.
14. iv. Sarah Edith Young was born December 21, 1911.

9. **Albert[4] Cooksey** (Timothy F.[3], Samuel[2], William[1]), was born December 3, 1885 in Illinois, and died 1961 in Illinois.
He married Ada, who was born about 1876 in Illinois, and died May 4, 1945 in Galesburg, Knox County, Illinois.

Children:
i. Margaret A.[5] Cooksey was born about 1914 in Knox County, Illinois, and died May 25, 1917 in Henderson Township, Knox County, Illinois.

10. **Walter Arthur[4] Cooksey** (George W.[3], Samuel[2], William[1]), was born April 9, 1901 in New Windsor, Mercer County, Illinois, and died March 22, 1974 in Davenport, Scott County, Iowa. He was buried March 1974 in Fairmount Cemetery, Davenport, Scott County, Iowa.[13]

Walter and Amy (McDowell) Cooksey headstone

He married Amy Ruth McDowell, who was October 8, 1902 in Henry County, Illinois (daughter of Aram Allen McDowell and Caroline Carlson), and died June 25, 1996. She was buried June 1996 in Fairmount Cemetery, Davenport, Scott County, Iowa.[14]

Children:

15.   i. Rose Pearl[5] Cooksey was born July 29, 1923.

        ii. Helen Cooksey was born July 14, 1925 in Galesburg, Knox County, Illinois, and died August 14, 2012 in Fort Madison, Lee County, Iowa. She was buried August 2012 in Fairmount Cemetery, Davenport, Scott County, Iowa.[15]

Helen Deethardt, 87, of Fort Madison, died at 5:05 a.m. Tuesday, August 14, 2012, at the Fort Madison Health Center in Fort Madison.

Born July 14, 1925, in Galesburg, she was the daughter of Walter A. and Amy Ruth McDowell Cooksey. She married Norman Deethardt. He died April 2, 2006.

Helen worked as an accountant for a financial group in Mount Pleasant.

She was a member of Concordia Lutheran Church. She was president of American Ladies Auxillary in Florida and past member of the Eastern Star. She enjoyed fishing in the ocean with her husband, cookouts in her backyard, and golfing.

Survivors include her brother, Walter A. Cooksey, Jr. of Rossville, GA; three nieces, Mary Jane (Richard) Huston of West Burlington, Lisa Cooksey, and Marlene Cooksey; three nephews, Jerry A. Lamb, Chris Cooksey, and Samuel Cooksey.

Besides her husband, she was preceded in death by her parents, one brother, George Cooksey, and two sisters, Rose White, and Maxine Mohler.

Burial will be in Fairmount Cemetery in Davenport.

Helen (Cooksey) Deethardt

Norman Deethardt

She married Norman Deethardt, who was born November 7, 1920, and died April 2, 2006. He was buried April 2006 in Fairmount Cemetery, Davenport, Scott County, Iowa.[16]

iii.   Myrtle Maxine Cooksey was born July 23, 1927 in Galesburg, Knox County, Illinois, and died April 12, 2012 in West Burlington, Des Moines County, Iowa.[17] She was buried April 2012 in Davenport Memorial Park, Davenport, Scott County, Iowa.[18]

Myrtle Maxine Mohler, 84, of Fort Madison, died at 4:20 pm Friday, April 13, 2012, at the Great River Hospice House in West Burlington.
Born July 23, 1927, in Galesburg, IL, she was the daughter of Walter A. and Amy Ruth McDowell Cooksey. On December 18, 1943, she married Anthony Joseph "Tony" Mohler in Galesburg, IL. He died March 7, 2005
Maxine and her husband Tony farmed in Union, Iowa. She also was a caregiver for her mother, a sitter for people in the nursing homes, and individuals in their own homes.
She was a member of Concordia Lutheran Church. She was confirmed on May 31, 1964. She enjoyed crocheting, gardening, and raised geese. She loved her little dog, Sammy, and reading her Bible.
Survivors include her sister, Helen Deethardt of Fort Madison; one brother, Walter A. Cooksey Jr. of Rossville, GA; her niece, Mary Jane (Richard) Huston of West Burlington, and other nieces, nephews, great-nieces and great-nephews.
Besides her husband, she was preceded in death by her parents, one brother George, and one sister Rose.
Interment will be in Davenport Memorial Park Cemetery.

She married Anthony Joseph Mohler, December 18, 1943 in Galesburg, Knox County, Illinois. He was born 1908, and died March 7, 2005, and buried March 2005 in Davenport Memorial Park, Davenport, Scott County, Iowa.[19]

Anthony Joseph "Tony" Mohler, 96, of Burlington, died at 2:47 PM, Monday, March 7, 2005 at the Great River Medical Center in West Burlington. Born September 20, 1908, in West Burlington, he was the son of Charles and Lena Fritz Mohler. On December 18, 1943, he married Myrtle "Maxine" Cooksey in Galesburg, IL. Mr. Mohler was a boiler maker for the CB&Q Railroad from 1917 until 1948. He was a Foreman of the Welding Department for the Innes Co. in Bettendorf for 15 years after which he worked for Rampco for 10 years and also at Caterpillar. He was a member of Concordia Lutheran Church and New London Country Club. He enjoyed gardening, flowers, and baseball, especially the Atlanta Braves. Survivors include his wife, Maxine; three sisters, Ruth Hingst and Jeanette Mosena, both of Burlington, and Doris Brenneman of West Burlington; and several nieces and nephews. He was preceded in death by his parents, two brothers, and two sisters. Interment in Davenport Memorial Park Cemetery in Davenport, Iowa.

iv.   Walter J. Cooksey was born about 1931 in Illinois.

v.   George Allen Cooksey was born August 30, 1932, and died November 28, 1995. He was buried December 1995 in Fairmount Cemetery, Davenport, Scott County, Iowa.[20]

George Allen Cooksey headstone

11. **Georgia Lucille[4] Cooksey** (George W.[3], Samuel[2], William[1]), was born February 1, 1908 in Aledo, Mercer County, Illinois, and died January 28, 1978 in Maquon, Knox County, Illinois.[21] She was buried February 1978 in Maquon Cemetery, Maquon, Knox County, Illinois.

Galesburg Register-Mail
Jan 1978
MRS. W. BAUGHMAN
MAQUON - Mrs. William (Georgia) Baughman, 69, of Maquon Route 2, died Tuesday at 5 a.m. at her house.
The former Georgia Cooksey was born Feb. 1, 1908 in Aledo, and married William P. Baughman on June 7, 1946 in Galesburg.
He survives with three sons, Eugene, Clarence and Wayne Briggs, all of Galesburg; two daughters, Mrs. Darlene Thompson, Wataga, and Mrs. Doris Thompson, of near Gilson; 22 grandchildren and nine great-grandchildren.
Funeral service will be Thursday at 2 p.m. at the Root Funeral Home, Maquon, where friends may call today from 6-8 p.m. Rev. Carroll Ochsner will officiate. Burial will be in the Maquon Cemetery.

She married Clarence Max Briggs, about 1924 in Illinois. He was born May 1, 1905 in Sparta Township, Knox County, Illinois,[22] (son of Francis Albert Briggs and Techla Sophia Erickson), and died March 9, 1960 in Galesburg, Knox County, Illinois.[23] He was buried March 12, 1960 in Maquon Cemetery, Maquon, Knox County, Illinois.[24]

OBITUARY FOR Clarence Briggs
(Galesburg Register-Mail 10 Mar 1960)

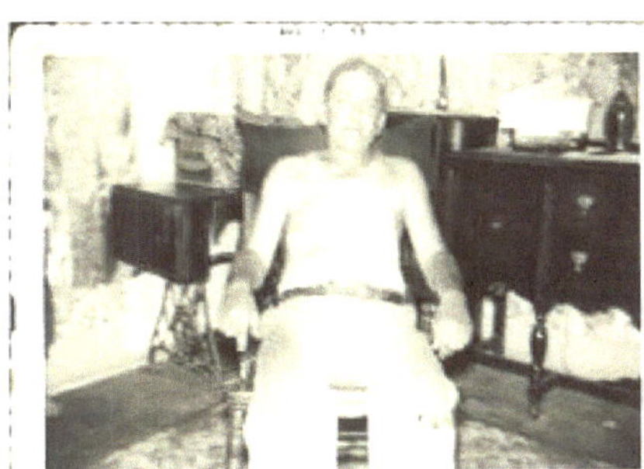

Clarence Max Briggs

CLARENCE BRIGGS MAQUON - Clarence Max Briggs, 55, of Maquon, died Wednesday at1:10 a.m. at St. Mary's Hospital in Galesburg. He had been a patient there for the past two weeks.
Mr. Briggs was born May 1, 1904 in Galesburg and lived here until five years ago when he moved to Maquon. He was a farmer. He married Miss Jennie Slagel in 1953 in Galesburg and she survives. Other survivors include three sons, Clarence Jr and Wayne Leroy,both of Galesburg, and Gene of Elba Center; two daughters, Mrs. Marian Thompson of Galesburg and Mrs. Darlene Thompson of Gilson; a brother Frank of Galesburg; two sisters, Mrs. Marian Welch and Mrs. Alta Boone, both of Galesburg; 16 grandchildren and several nieces and nephews.
Funeral services will be Saturday at 2 p.m. at the Methodist Church in Maquon. Friends may call at the Root-Davis Funeral Home after 4 p.m. Friday. Burial will be in Maquon Cemetery.

Children:

16.   i. Eugene Allen[5] Briggs was born October 9, 1925.

          ii. Betty Irene Briggs was born December 10, 1928 in Soperville, Knox County, Illinois,[25] and died September 4, 1937 in Galesburg, Knox County, Illinois.[26] She was buried September 1937 in Memorial Park Cemetery, Galesburg, Knox County, Illinois.[27]

Betty Irene Briggs' death certificate

Galesburg Daily Register
4 Sep 1937
BETTY BRIGGS, EIGHT YEARS OLD, VICTIM OF TRAGIC ACCIDENT;
VEHICLE BACKS OVER BODY
Automobile accidents claimed the sixteenth Knox county victim this year and the second to die in Galesburg when Betty Briggs, eight-year-old daughter of Mr and Mrs Clarence Briggs 956 Yates street,was run over and killed at 7:25 this morning just south of the Morton avenue and Yates street intersection by a Golden Cream dairy truck driven by M.M. Herndon, 67 North Farnham street. Mr. Herndon was delivering milk on his route when the fatal accident occurred. He was driving south on Morton avenue, next to the Rio tracks of the C.B. and Q railroad, and had gone a hundred feet past Yates street before stopping to deliver milk to a woman customer. The driver started to back his truck up to Yates street to resume his route, but felt the vehicle pass over an object, and he observed a young girl screaming "Oh, Betty," putting her hands to her eyes. He stopped the truck immediately and alighted to find the young victim of the accident run over by the truck and apparently hit by a rear bolt on the wagon. The city ambulance was called to the scene, but the child was pronounced dead shortly after arrival at Galesburg Cottage Hospital. Betty Briggs was the daughter of Clarence and Georgia Briggs. She leaves her parents; the following brothers and sisters, Eugene, Marion, Junior Albert, Darlene and Wayne; her grandmother, Mrs. Hettie Engle; and her grandfather, Albert Briggs. Funeral rites will be held at 10 o'clock, Monday morning, from the Dean Funeral home. Dr. G. S. Bower, coroner, conducted an inquest at one o'clock this afternoon in the funeral home.

17.   iii. Marion Maxine Briggs was born April 14, 1930.

18.   iv. Clarence Albert Briggs was born April 30, 1932.

19.   v. Darlene Briggs was born May 2, 1933.

        vi. Wayne Leroy Briggs was born April 16, 1936 in Galesburg, Knox County, Illinois, and died July 19, 1994 in Galesburg, Knox County, Illinois. He was buried July 1994 in Maquon Cemetery, Maquon, Knox County, Illinois.

Wayne Leroy Briggs

Ruth (Smelser) Briggs headstone

He married Ruth Smelser, who was born April 12, 1934 in Knox County, Illinois, and died January 25, 1986 in Galesburg, Knox County, Illinois. She was buried January 1986 in Walnut Grove Cemetery, Altona, Knox County, Illinois.[28]

20.   vii. Doris M. Briggs b. September 1938.

Generation Five

12. **Martha Tracy[5] Young** (William Frank[4], Sarah Ann[3] Cooksey, Samuel[2], William[1]), was born October 9, 1901 in New Windsor, Mercer County, Illinois, and died October 25, 1971 in Moline, Rock Island County, Illinois. She was buried October 1971 in Rose Lawn Memorial Estate, Moline, Rock Island County, Illinois.
She married Ralph Charles Johnson, who was born July 24, 1900 in Andover, Henry County, Illinois, and died December 20, 1976 in Milan, Rock Island County, Illinois. He was buried December 1976 in Rose Lawn Memorial Estate, Moline, Rock Island County, Illinois.[29]

> *Children:*
> i. Robert R.[6] Johnson.

13. **William Horace[5] Young** (William Frank[4], Sarah Ann[3] Cooksey, Samuel[2], William[1]), was born December 26, 1905 in New Windsor, Mercer County, Illinois, and diedOctober 29, 1988 in Mesa, Maricopa County, Arizona.
He married Louise Miller.

> *Children:*
> i. Horace Earle[6] Young was born November 12, 1931 in Moline, Rock Island County, Illinois, and died. May 11, 1965 in Contoocook, Merrimack County, New Hampshire. He was buried May 1965 in Rock Island National Cemetery, Rock Island, Rock Island County, Illinois.[30]

Horace Earle Young

Horace Young's headstone

14. **Sarah Edith[5] Young** (William Frank[4], Sarah Ann[3] Cooksey, Samuel[2], William[1]), was born December 21, 1911 in New Windsor, Mercer County, Illinois, and died November 8, 1988 in Geneseo, Henry County, Illinois. She was, buried November 1988 in Andover Township Cemetery, Andover, Henry County, Illinois.[31] *Sarah and Chester were the parents of four children.*

Sarah Edith (Young) Johnson and Chester Johnson

She married Chester August Johnson, who was born July 4, 1902 in Andover, Henry County, Illinois, and died June 26, 1985 in Geneseo, Henry County, Illinois. He was buried June 1985 in Andover Township Cemetery, Andover, Henry County, Illinois.[32]

> *Children:*
> i. Chester Clyde[6] Johnson b. April 6, 1932 in Moline, Rock Island County, Illinois, d. April 9, 1932 in Moline, Rock Island County, Illinois.
> ii. Donald Chester Johnson b. September 21, 1933, d. November 4, 1934 in Milan, Rock Island County, Illinois.

15. **Rose Pearl[5] Cooksey** (Walter Arthur[4], George W.[3], Samuel[2], William[1]), was born July 29, 1923 in Viola, Mercer County, Illinois, and died February 26, 2002 in Iowa City, Johnson County, Iowa. She was buried March 2002 in Fairmont Cemetery, Davenport, Scott County, Iowa.[33]

Rose P. White, age 78 of Burlington passed away at 7:05 AM Tuesday, February 26, 2002 at the University of Iowa Hospitals and Clinics in Iowa City.
Born July 29, 1923 in Viola, IL she was the daughter of Walter A. and Amy Ruth McDowell Cooksey. She married Gerald Lamb in 1940 in Galesburg, IL. They later divorced. He died in 1963. She then married Lloyd M. White in 1954 in Burlington. He died in 1982.
Mrs. White went to grade school in Galesburg and then to Churchill High School in Galesburg and then went on to become a Licensed Practical Nurse. She was a Licensed Practical Nurse at Monmouth Hospital and in private homes. She was a member of St. Paul?s Lutheran Church in Wapello and the American Legion Auxiliary for 30 years. She was an avid Iowa Hawkeye?s fan, loved to cook, help people, enjoyed friends, and her church and loved spending time with her grandchildren.
Survivors include one son, Jerry Allen Lamb of Larnie, Ireland; one daughter, Mary J. Huston of West Burlington; six grandchildren; 25 great grandchildren; one brother, Walter J. Cooksey of Graysville, Georgia; two sisters, Helen Deethardt and Maxine Mohler both of Burlington; and eight nieces and nephews. Besides her husbands she was preceded in death by her parents and one younger brother.

She married (1) Gerald Lamb, 1940 in Galesburg, Knox County, Illinois. He died 1963.

> *Children:*
> i. Jerry Allen[6] Lamb.
> ii. Mary J. Lamb.

Lloyd and Rose Pearl (Cooksey) White headstone

She married (2) Lloyd P. White, 1954 in Burlington, Iowa. He died 1982.

16. **Eugene Allen[5] Briggs** (Georgia Lucille[4] Cooksey, George W.[3], Samuel[2], William[1]), was born October 9, 1925 in Elba Center Township, Knox County, Illinois,[34] and died July 15, 1988 in Galesburg, Knox County, Illinois,[35] (cause of death chronic obstructive pulminary disease). He was buried July 18, 1988 in Memorial Park Cemetery, Galesburg, Knox County, Illinois.[36] *He was married before Bonnie E. Pratt but they had no children and divorced. He was a carpenter and worked at various home repair jobs throughout his life. At one time he was in business with his brother Clarence with a home repair business in and around Galesburg, Knox County, Illinois.*

Eugene Allen Briggs and Bonnie Eugenie Pratt (and marriage certificate)

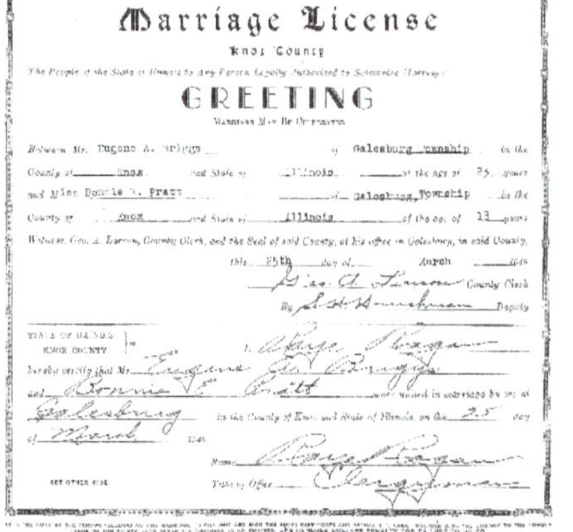

He married Bonnie Eugenie Pratt, March 25, 1949 in Galesburg, Knox County, Illinois.[37] She was born April 9, 1930 in Smithshire, Warren County, Illinois (daughter of Edgar Leroy Pratt and Eleanor "Nellie" Jones), and died January 3, 2014 in Galesburg, Knox County, Illinois. She was buried January 10, 2014 in Monmouth Cemetery, (old) Warren County, Illinois.[38]

   Children:
21. i. Eugene Allen[6] Briggs, Jr. was born April 7, 1950.
22. ii. Joyce Marie Briggs was born June 6, 1951.
23. iii. Beverly Ann Briggs was born May 15, 1952.
24. iv. Mary Louise Briggs was born September 29, 1953.

17. **Marion Maxine[5] Briggs** (Georgia Lucille[4] Cooksey, George W.[3], Samuel[2], William[1]), was born April 14, 1930 in Galesburg, Knox County, Illinois,[39] and died August 29, 1963 in Galesburg, Knox County, Illinois,[40] (cause of death acute leukemia). She was buried August 31, 1963 in Memorial Park Cemetery, Galesburg, Knox County, Illinois.[41]

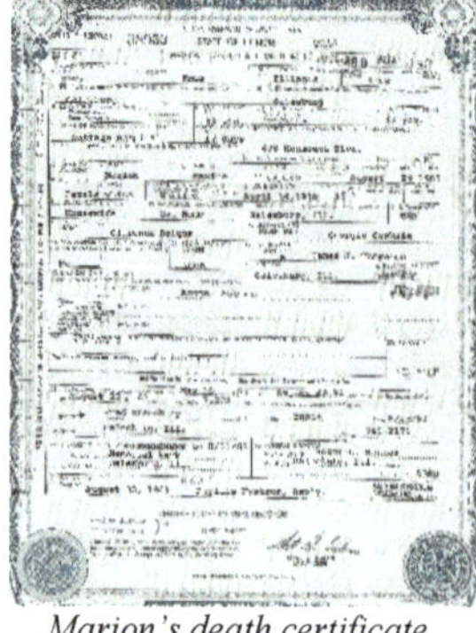

| Marion Maxine (Briggs) Thompson | Marion's death certificate | Jame Thompson's headstone |

She married James J. Thompson, January 8, 1958 in Galesburg, Knox County, Illinois. He was born September 4, 1928 in Victoria, Knox County, Illinois, and died December 16, 1993 in Galesburg, Knox County, Illinois. He was buried December 22, 1993 in Maquon Cemetery, Maquon, Knox County, Illinois.

Peoria Journal Star, The (IL) -
December 18, 1993
Deceased Name: JAMES THOMPSON
GALESBURG -- James J. Thompson, 65, of 116 Kimberly Terrace died at 10:23 a.m. Thursday, Dec. 16, 1993, at Galesburg Cottage Hospital.
Born Sept. 4, 1928, in Victoria to James and Maxine Decker Thompson, he married Doris Briggs on June 18, 1993, in Gilson. She survives.
Also surviving are one son, Jimmie Thompson of Monmouth; one daughter, Patricia Massachusetts of Texas; two stepsons, John Thompson of Knoxville and Steve Thompson of Dahinda; two stepdaughters, Lou Ann and Sharon Thompson, both of Gilson; three brothers,David and Virgil, both of Galesburg, and Thomas of Galva; three sisters, Ethel Caldwell and Loreta Wells, both of Galesburg, and Betty Patrick of Normal; and 12 grandchildren.
He was a Korean War Army veteran.
He was a molder for the Iowa Malleable Co.
Graveside services will be at 11 a.m. Tuesday at Maquon Cemetery in Maquon. The Rev. T. Richard Bilyea Jr. will officiate. Visitation will be from 6 to 8 p.m. Monday at Root Funeral Home in Maquon.

      Children:
- i.   Roddy Lee[6] Thompson. *He was her son born before James' children. Officially raised by his grandmother Georgia Baughman.*
- ii.   Patricia Ann Thompson.
- 25.   iii.   James Allen Thompson.
- iv.   Rodney Dean Thompson was born August 29, 1963 in Galesburg, Knox County, Illinois, and died September 1963 in Galesburg, Knox County, Illinois, buried September 1963 in Memorial Park Cemetery, Galesburg, Knox County, Illinois. *He was born the day his mother died of leukemia. He must have known she was gone as he didn't live that long after her death. I remember that even though I was barely 9 at that time.*

Rodney Dean Thompson headstone

18. **Clarence Albert[5] Briggs** (Georgia Lucille[4] Cooksey, George W.[3], Samuel[2], William[1]), was born April 30, 1932 in Knox County, Illinois, and died June 1981 in Galesburg, Knox County, Illinois.

Clarence Albert Briggs

Clarence "Junior" Briggs was born April 30, 1932 to Clarence Max and Georgia Lucille Cooksey Briggs.
He married Donna E. Cook in Galesburg May 15, 1954.
His wife survives along with one son, James (and Gloria) Briggs, and two daughters, Mrs. Mary Morris and Mrs. Catherine Miller; and one sister Doris Thompson of Galesburg.
Besides his parents preceding him in death, he also lost two brothers, Wayne and Eugene, and three sisters, Marian, Betty and Darlene.
He was a self-employed repair contractor with his brother Gene for over 20 years. He served in the U.S. Army during the Korean War.

He married Donna E. Cook, May 15, 1954 in Galesburg, Knox County, Illinois.

   Children:
26. i. James[6] Briggs.
   ii. Mary Ellen Briggs.
     She married 'unknown' Morris. Married twice but second spouse unknown.
   iii. Catherine Briggs.
     She married Bruce Miller. She also married again and was living in Peoria, Illinois.

19. **Darlene**[5] **Briggs** (Georgia Lucille[4] Cooksey, George W.[3], Samuel[2], William[1]), was born May 2, 1933 in Knox County, Illinois, and died July 23, 1980 in Wataga, Knox County, Illinois. She was buried July 1980 in Wataga Cemetery, Wataga, Knox County, Illinois.

WATAGA -- Mrs. Darlene Thompson, 47, Wataga, died at home Wednesday at 5:40 a.m.
She was born May 2, 1933, in Knox County. She married Arnold C. Thompson Nov. 19, 1953, in Galesburg.
Surviving are her husband; a daughter, Mrs. Ricky (Carol) Morris, Wataga; seven sons, Robert Briggs, Eugene Thompson, Arnold Thompson, Jr., and Don Thompson, all of Galesburg, Jerry Thompson, East Galesburg, and Jimmy Thompson and Billy Thompson, both of Wataga; a sister, Mrs. Robert (Doris) Thompson, Maquon; three brothers, Eugene Briggs, Clarence Briggs and Wayne Briggs, all of Galesburg, and nine grandchildren.
Funeral will be Friday at 1:30 p.m. in Hurd-Hendricks Funeral Home, Knoxville, where friends may call Thursday from 7-9 p.m. Burial will be in Wataga Cemetery.
Memorials may be made to the Heart Fund, the family said.

She married Arnold C. Thompson, November 19, 1953 in Galesburg, Knox County, Illinois.[42] He was born October 27, 1932 in Victoria, Knox County, Illinois,[43] and died July 23, 1980 in Galesburg, Knox County, Illinois.[44] He was buried July 1980 in Wataga Cemetery, Wataga, Knox County, Illinois.[45]

Arnold C. Thompson Sr., 59, of 170 W. Simmons died at 9:50 a.m. Wednesday, Aug. 5, 1992, at Cottage Hospital in Galesburg.
Born Oct. 27, 1932, in rural Victoria, he married Darlene Briggs on Nov. 19, 1953, in Galesburg. She died July 23, 1980. He also was preceded in death by nine brothers and sisters.
Surviving are one daughter, Mrs. Carol Sue Morris of Galesburg; six sons, Eugene Thompson of Maquon, Junior Thompson and Jimmy Thompson, both of Galesburg, Don Thompson of Rock Island, Jerry Thompson of East Galesburg and Billy Thompson of Abingdon; one stepson, Robert Briggs of St. Augustine; 15 grandchildren; seven stepgrandchildren; three sisters, Ethel Cadwell and Loretta Wells, both of Galesburg, and Betty Patrick of Bloomington; and four brothers, Tom and Dave, both of Galva, and James and Virgil, both of Galesburg.
He was raised and educated in the Victoria area and was a farmer. He also was a molder at the Galva Foundry and the Aluminum Castings Co., in Galesburg.
Graveside services will be at 1 p.m. Saturday at Wataga Cemetery. The Rev. Milton Marquith will officiate. Visitation will be from 7 to 8:30 tonight at Hurd-Hendricks Funeral Home in Knoxville.

Children:
i. Robert Mahnesmith[6] Briggs was born December 25, 1951 in Galesburg, Knox County, Illinois, and died March 9, 2008 in Galesburg, Knox County, Illinois. He was buried March 2008 in Maquon Cemetery, Macquon, Knox County, Illinois.[46] *his stepfather was Arnold C. Thompson but he was mainly raised by his grandmother.*

Robert L. Briggs, age 56, of 1459 South Kellogg Street, Galesburg, Illinois died on Sunday, March 9, 2008 at 1:20 P.M. at his residence.
He was born on December 25, 1951 in Galesburg, Illinois, the son of Darlene Lois Briggs.
Surviving are one brother, Eugene L. (Floris) Thompson of Maquon, Illinois; four halfbrothers, Junior (Sharon) Thompson of Galesburg, Illinois, Don Thompson of Rock Island, Illinois, Jerry (Mary) Thompson

of East Galesburg, Illinois and Billie Thompson of Galesburg, Illinois; one halfsister, Carol Morris of Galesburg, Illinois; one aunt, Doris Thompson of Galesburg, Illinois; several nieces and nephews and great nieces and great nephews; and special friends, Bud and Pam Starnes of Maquon, Illinois. He was preceded by his parents; one halfbrother: Jimmie Thompson and his grandparents: Georgie and Bill Baughman who raised him.

He was born and raised in Williamsfield and Maquon, Illinois. He worked at Butler Manufacturing as a welder and in the maintenance department. He then worked at Mid-State Manufacturing in Galesburg, Illinois. He was active in the reenactment of Heritage Days in Galesburg, Illinois and attended other reenactments throughout the year. He was an active follower of the National Hot Rod Association and was an active fisherman.

Cremation Rites will be accorded. Memorial Services will be held on Saturday, March 15, 2008 at 1:00 P.M. at the Hurd Hendricks Funeral Home and Crematory in Knoxville, Illinois. Rev. Marilyn Anell officiating. Visitation will be held on Saturday, March 15, 2008 from 11:00 A.M. until time of services at the Funeral Home in Knoxville, Illinois. Inurnment in Maquon Cemetery in Maquon, Illinois. Memorials may be made to the Family.

27.   ii.   Donald W. Thompson was born February 9, 1956.
28.   iii.   Carol Sue Thompson was born March 12, 1957.
29.   iv.   Jerry D. Thompson was born March 12, 1958.
30.   v.   James Thompson was born April 6, 1960.
       vi.   Eugene Thompson.
           He married Florence.
      vii.   Arnold Thompson.
           He married Sharon.
    viii.   William Thompson.
           He married Sally.

20. **Doris M.[5] Briggs** (Georgia Lucille[4] Cooksey, George W.[3], Samuel[2], William[1]), was born September 1938 in Knox County, Illinois, and died October 26, 2016 in Galesburg, Knox County, Illinois, buried October 2016 in Maquon Cemetery, Maquon, Knox County, Illinois.[47]
She married Robert Thompson. He was born June 14, 1960 and died January 31, 1985. He is buried in Maquon Cemetery, Maquon, Knox County, Illinois.

    Children:
    i.   Sharon[6] Thompson was born 1960
    ii.   Karen Thompson was born 1960 (twin of Sharon Thompson) and died February 26, 1960. She is buried in Maquon Cemetery, Maquon, Knox County, Illinois.

Karen Thompson headstone

    iii.   John Thompson.
    iv.   Steve Thompson.
    v.   Louann Thompson.

Generation Six

21. **Eugene Allen[6] Briggs, Jr.** (Eugene Allen[5], Georgia Lucille[4] Cooksey, George W.[3], Samuel[2], William[1]), was born April 7, 1950 in Galesburg, Knox County, Illinois.

Eugene Allen Briggs, Jr ,   *Sherry Kiddy,*   *Adam Briggs,*   *Aaron Briggs*   *, Alyssa Briggs*

He married (1) Sherry Kiddy.

> *Children:*
> 31. i. William "Billie"[7] Briggs.
> 32. ii. Bobbi Jo Briggs.

He married (2) Lorie Marie Horn, December 1, 1980 in Schuyler County, Missouri.[48]

> *Children:*
> iii. Michael Briggs.
> iv. Adam Joseph Briggs.
> v. Aaron Moses Briggs.
> vi. Alyssa Marcella Marie Briggs.

22. **Joyce Marie[6] Briggs** (Eugene Allen[5], Georgia Lucille[4] Cooksey, George W.[3], Samuel[2], William[1]), b. June 6, 1951 in Galesburg, Knox County, Illinois.

She married (1) Harley Matheny.

> *Children:*
> 33. i. Georgia Marie[7] Matheny.
> 34. ii. Robert Eugene Matheny b. September 13, 1970.
> 35. iii. Steven Lee Matheny.

She married (2) Homer Gordon Cox, November 3, 1979 in Galesburg, Knox County, Illinois. He was born June 3, 1933 in Illinois, and died July 7, 2009 in Illinois. He was buried July 10, 2009 in Oak Lawn Memorial Gardens, Galesburg, Knox County, Illinois.

GALESBURG - Homer Gordon Cox, 76, 1722 S. Cherry St., Galesburg, died at 4:05 a.m. Tuesday, July 7, 2009, in Kindred Hospital, Sycamore.
He was born June 3, 1933, in Kirkwood, the son of Otis Gordon and Zetta Mae Owens Cox. He married Joyce Marie Briggs on Nov. 3, 1979, in Galesburg.

He is survived by his special friend, Joyce Cox of Galesburg, and a son, Joshua D. Cox of Galesburg. He was preceded in death by his parents, two brothers and a sister.
Homer was a welder for Bixby Zimmer for 19 years, retiring in 1996. He graduated from Monmouth High School. He was a member of First Christian Church, Moose Lodge 880 and the former Eagle's Lodge. Homer sang and was lead guitarist in the band Virginia Plus.
He served in the United States Navy during the Korean War.
Visitation will be 9 to 10:30 a.m. Friday at Hinchliff-Pearson-West Galesburg Chapel. Burial will follow at Oak Lawn Memorial Gardens, with Captain Rick Ray officiating. Military rites will be provided by Ralph M. Noble American Legion Post 285. Memorials may be made to the family. Online condolences may be made at www.h-p-w.com.
Published in The Register-Mail on 7/9/2009.

Joyce Marie (Briggs) Wright

Homer Gordon Cox

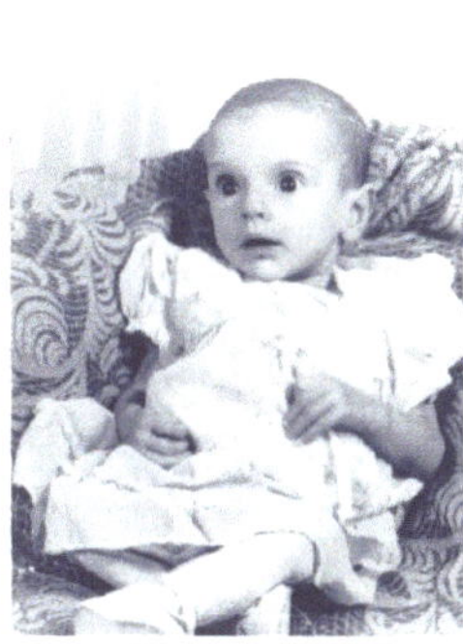

Joyce Cox-Wright

William Wright

    Children:
   iv. Joshua David Cox.

She married (3) William Wright.

23. **Beverly Ann**[6] **Briggs** (Eugene Allen[5], Georgia Lucille[4] Cooksey, George W.[3], Samuel[2], William[1]), was born May 15, 1952 in Galesburg, Knox County, Illinois, and died January 29, 1995 in Galesburg, Knox County, Illinois. She was buried February 1, 1995 in Monmouth Cemetery (old), Warren County, Illinois.

Beverly Ann (Briggs) Meehan

Larue James Meehan

Some of the current Meehan family

OBITUARY for Beverly A. Meehan
Galesburg Register-Mail
Jan. 31, 1995
BEVERLY A. MEEHAN MONMOUTH -- Beverly Ann Meehan, 42, 315 S. Fifth St., died at11:30 p.m. Sunday (Jan. 29, 1995) at her sister's home in Galesburg. She was born May 15, 1952, in Galesburg, the daughter of Eugene A. and Bonnie E. Briggs Sr. She married LaRue J. Meehan on Oct. 20, 1972, in Galesburg. Surviving are her husband; her mother, Bonnie E. Briggs, Galesburg; three daughters, Wanita J. Meehan, Crystal L. Meehan and MichelleR. Meehan, all of Monmouth; three sons,

Patrick L. Meehan and DavidL. Meehan, both of Monmouth, and LaRue J. Meehan Jr., in the U.S.Army in South Korea; one stepson, Anthony R. Meehan, Burlington, Iowa;two sisters, Joyce M. Cox, Galesburg, and Mary L. Moeller, Carpentersville, and one brother, Eugene A. Briggs Jr., Galesburg. She was reared in Galesburg, and was graduated from Galesburg High School.
She was a homemaker.
She was a member of Grace Bible Church, Monmouth. Funeral will be at 10 a.m. Wednesday in Turnbull Funeral Home, Monmouth.Friends may call at the funeral home today and Wednesday until theservice; the family will be present from 7 to 8:30 p.m. today. Burial will be in Monmouth Cemetery.

She married (1) Lindal Paul, was born January 1948 in Illinois.
She married (2) Larue James Meehan, October 20, 1972 in Galesburg, Knox County, Illinois. He was September 1943 in Illinois. [49]

        Children:

36.	i.	Larue James[7] Meehan II b. April 1974.
37.	ii.	Wanita Meehan.
38.	iii.	Patrick Meehan.
	iv.	David Meehan.
		He married Amber Carter.
39.	v.	Crystal Meehan.
	vi.	Michelle Meehan.

24. **Mary Louise[6] Briggs** (Eugene Allen[5], Georgia Lucille[4] Cooksey, George W.[3], Samuel[2], William[1]), was born September 29, 1953 in Monmouth, Warren County, Illinois.
    She married (1) Dennis Mark Ashby, May 8, 1976 in Galesburg, Knox County, Illinois. He was born May 5, 1953 in Chicago, Cook County, Illinois (son of Mark Olin Ashby and Mildred Bernice Holzschuh). Dennis: Married but currently divorced.

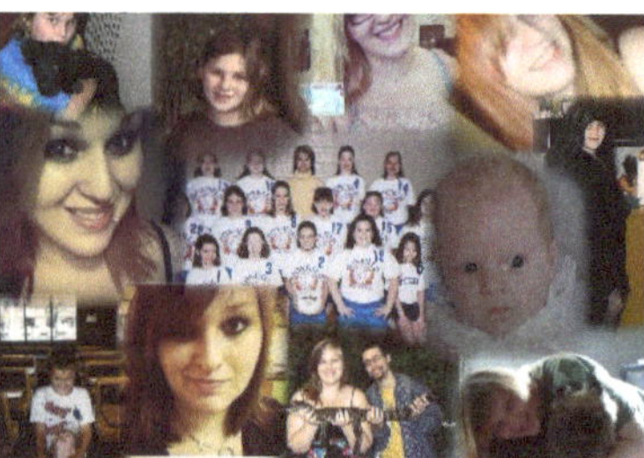

Mary Louise (Briggs) Moeller   Mary and Dennis Ashby   Kevin Scott Ashby   Jessica Jaime Devon Moeller

Ronald Robinson   Russell Kelly

He worked for many many years as a machinist making precision drill bits. Only one child and that is Kevin Scott Ashby.

        Children:

i. Kevin Scott[7] Ashby b. July 10, 1985 in Elgin, Kane County, Illinois.[50]

She married (2) Randy Scott Moeller, was born October 4, 1961 in Saint Charles, Kane County, Illinois.

Children:
ii. Jessica Jaime Devon Moeller b. August 11, 1992 in Geneva, Kane County, Illinois.

25. **James Allen[6] Thompson** (Marion Maxine[5] Briggs, Georgia Lucille[4] Cooksey, George W.[3], Samuel[2], William[1]), died in July 2008 in Connerville, Oklahoma.
He married Paula Day.

Paula Day and children

Children:
40. i. Stefanie Marie[7] Thompson.
41. ii. Melanie Thompson.
42. iii. Adam James "Thompson" Swindell.

26. **James[6] Briggs** (Clarence Albert[5], Georgia Lucille[4] Cooksey, George W.[3], Samuel[2], William[1]).
He married Gloria June Horn.

Children:
i. Caitlynn Anne[7] Briggs.

27. **Donald W.[6] Thompson** (Darlene[5] Briggs, Georgia Lucille[4] Cooksey, George W.[3], Samuel[2], William[1]), was born February 9, 1956 in Galesburg, Knox County, Illinois, and died October 24, 2014 in Qquawka, Henderson County, Illinois. He was buried October 2014 in Wataga Cemetery, Wataga, Knox County, Illinois.[51]

Donald W. Thompson

OQUAWKA - Don W. Thompson, 58, Oquawka, formerly of Wataga and Rock Island, died at 7:03 a.m. Friday, Oct. 24, 2014, at his home in Oquawka. His life was fulfilled with being a giver.

He was born Feb. 9, 1956, in Galesburg, the son of Arnold and Darlene Briggs Thompson. He married Karen Wright in 1976 in Galesburg.

He leaves behind two daughters, Alisha (Rachel Fye) Fues of Oquawka, and Marsha (Patrick) Yerkey of Keller, Texas; one loving grandson, Damien and two beautiful granddaughters, Alexis and Sarah; three brothers, Junior (Sharon) Thompson of Galesburg, Billy Thompson of Galesburg, Eugene (Florence) Briggs of Maquon; and many nieces and nephews. He was preceded in death by his parents, three brothers, and one sister. He will be sadly missed but always loved.

He owned and operated the Stop In Bar and Grill in Rock Island, cooked at the Ribco Bar and Grill in Rock Island, and then finally worked at the Isle of Capri in Rock Island, for many years.

He loved long walks, cooking, being outdoors, watching humming birds, riding on the golf cart, gambling and spending time with his family.

Funeral will be at 11 a.m. Tuesday, Oct. 28, 2014, at Hurd-Hendricks Funeral Homes in Knoxville. Visitation will be 5 to 7 p.m. Monday, Oct. 27, 2014, at Hurd-Hendricks Funeral Homes in Knoxville. Interment will take place at the Wataga Cemetery, Wataga. Fellowship will be at Hurd-Hendricks Fellowship Center following the services at the cemetery. Memorials may be made to the Knox County Humane Society. Online condolences and sympathy cards may be sent through www.hurd-hendricksfuneralhome.com.

He married Karen Wright, 1976 in Galesburg, Knox County, Illinois.

> *Children:*
> i. Marsha[7] Thompson.
>   *She married Patrick Yerkey.*
> ii. Alisha Thompson.

28. **Carol Sue[6] Thompson** (Darlene[5] Briggs, Georgia Lucille[4] Cooksey, George W.[3], Samuel[2], William[1]), was born March 12, 1957 in Galesburg, Knox County, Illinois, and died July 12, 2010 in Galesburg, Knox County, Illinois. He was buried July 2010 in Wataga Cemetery, Wataga, Knox County, Illinois.[52]

3/12/1957 - 7/12/2010

Carol Sue Morris, 53, of Galesburg, died at 11:50 p.m. Monday, July 12, 2010 at home.

Carol was born on March 12, 1957 in Galesburg the daughter of Arnold and Darlene (Briggs) Thompson. She is survived by two sons, Michael Thompson of Peoria and Mark Thompson of hicago; a daughter, Stacy (Travis Anderson) of Galesburg; 5 brothers, Arnold (Sharon) Thompson, Jr. of Galesburg, Jerry (Mary) Thompson of East Galesburg, Eugene (Florence) Briggs of Gilson, Billy (Sally) Thompson of Galesburg, and Don Thompson of Rock Island. Also surviving are 4 grandchildren, Noah and Lexi Anderson and Jareth and Conor Buckert-Anderson, and many nieces and nephews. She is preceded in death by her parents, two brothers, Jim Thompson and Bobby Briggs, and a nephew, Jimmy Thompson Jr.

Carol worked at Marigold Healthcare Center as a CNA for many years. She loved crossword puzzles, being in her backyard by her fire, going to casinos, and being with her family.

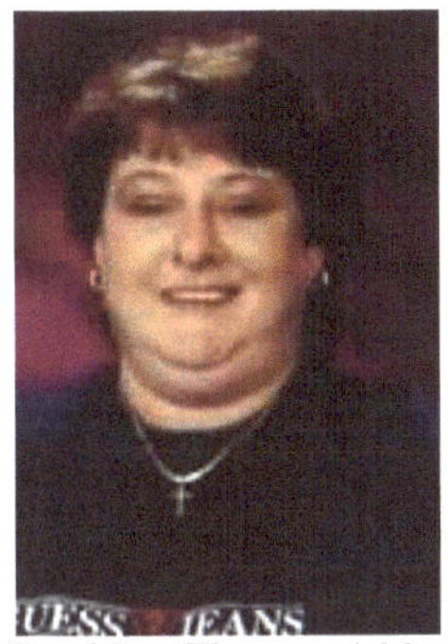

Carol Sue (Thompson) Morris   *Richard Morris*

She married Richard L. Morris, who was born February 27, 1955 in Galesburg, Knox County, Illinois, and died June 5, 2012 in Peoria, Peoria County, Illinois. He was buried June 2012 in Wataga Cemetery, Wataga, Knox County, Illinois.[53]

Richard: Rick L. Morris, Galesburg Chapel 57, of Monmouth, Ill died at 4:02 pm Thursday, June 5, 2012 in OSF St. Francis Medical Center in Peoria, Ill.
He was born February 27, 1955 in Galesburg the son of Floyd Robert Morris and Mary Louise Tracy Morris Foster. He married Carol Thompson in 1976. He later married Ann (Denly) Howell on July 2, 1997 in Monmouth, Ill. She survives. Also surviving is his daughter, Stacy (Travis) Anderson of Galesburg, step daughter, Joey Howell of Monmouth, Ill.; four brothers, Robert Leon (Mary) Morris of Monmouth, Ill, Floyd "Smoky" (Mary) Morris, Phil (Cindy) Morris, and Lawrence (Brenda) Morris all of Galesburg; five sisters, Judy (Kenny) Davis of Galesburg, Carol Bohannan of Gilson, Ill., Joyce Reading, Susan (Daniel) Sargeant both of Galesburg and Sarah (Casper) Kasparie of Knoxville, Ill., and five grandchildren, Kylee, Noah, Lexi, Jareth and Conor and many nieces and nephews survive. He is preceded in death by his parents and a brother Roger.
Rick worked as a mechanic. He enjoyed his life, loved to camp, loved his family and his dog.
Graveside services are scheduled for 1:30 pm Friday, June 8, 2012 in Wataga Cemetery. Rev. James Epperson will officiate. Visitation will be 12:00-1:00 pm Friday at Hinchliff-Pearson-West Galesburg Chapel. Memorials may be made to the family. Online condolences may be made at www.h-p-w.com.

> *Children:*
> i. Michael[7] Thompson.
> ii. Mark Thompson.
> iii. Stacy Morris.
> *She married Travis Anderson.*

29. **Jerry D.[6] Thompson** (Darlene[5] Briggs, Georgia Lucille[4] Cooksey, George W.[3], Samuel[2], William[1]), was born March 12, 1958 in Galesburg, Knox County, Illinois, and died May 1, 2011 in East Galesburg, Knox County, Illinois, cremated May 2011 in location of ashes unknown.

EAST GALESBURG - Jerry D. Thompson, 53, East Galesburg, died at 1:45 p.m. Sunday, May 1, 2011, at home.
He was born March 12, 1958, in Galesburg, the son of Arnold and Darlene Briggs Thompson. He married Mary E. Lufkin on Nov. 4, 1991, in East Galesburg.
Surviving are two sons, Jeremy (Lisa) Thompson of Galesburg and Shawn Thompson of East Galesburg; and four brothers, Jr. (Sharon) Thompson of Galesburg, Eugene (Floris) Briggs of Gilson, Don Thompson of Rock Island and Bill Thompson of Galesburg.

He was preceded in death by his parents; two brothers, Bob Briggs and Jim Thompson; one sister, Carol Morris; and one nephew, Jim Thompson Jr.
He was raised and educated in the Maquon and Wataga areas.
He worked as a contractor for The Galesburg Register-Mail for 23 years.
Cremation rites will be accorded. There will be no services. Memorials may be made to the family. Hurd-Hendricks Funeral Homes & Crematory is in charge of arrangements.
Online condolences or sympathy cards may be sent through www.hurd-hendricksfuneralhome.com.

He married Mary E. Lufkin, November 4, 1991 in East Galesburg, Knox County, Illinois.

> *Children:*
>   i.   Jeremy[7] Thompson.
>   *He married Lisa.*
> 43.   ii. Shawn Dustin Thompson b. June 24, 1981.

30. **James[6] Thompson** (Darlene[5] Briggs, Georgia Lucille[4] Cooksey, George W.[3], Samuel[2], William[1]), was born April 6, 1960 in Galesburg, Knox County, Illinois, and died April 25, 2004 in Peoria, Peoria County, Illinois. He was buried April 2004 in Wataga Cemetery, Wataga, Knox County, Illinois.[54]

Peoria Journal Star, April 27, 2004
GALESBURG- Jimmy A. Thompson, Sr., 44, of Galesburg died at 9:50 p.m. Sunday, April 25, 2004, at OSF Saint Francis Medical Center
in Peoria.
He was born April 6, 1960, in Galesburg to Arnold Sr. and Darlene Briggs Thompson.
Surviving are two sons, Jimmy Jr. and Joshua, both of Galesburg;one stepdaughter, Delilah "DeeDee" (and Sam) Hill of Maryville,Tenn.; one sister, Carol Morris of Galesburg; and six brothers, Billy Thompson, Arnold Jr. (and Sharon) Thompson and Robert Briggs,all of Galesburg, Jerry (and Mary) Thompson of East Galesburg,
Don Thompson of Rock Island and Eugene (and Doris) Briggs of Maquon; and his fiancee, Wanda Strahlman of Galesburg.
He was preceded in death by his parents.
He was a driver/carrier for The Register-Mail for six years.
Graveside services will be at 10 a.m. Thursday at Wataga Cemetery in Wataga. The Rev. Milton Marquith will officiate.
Visitation will be from 6 to 8 p.m. Wednesday at Hurd-Hendricks Funeral Home in Knoxville.

He married 'unknown'.

> *Children:*
>   i.   James[7] Thompson.
>   ii. Joshua Thompson.

Generation Seven

31. **William "Billie"[7] Briggs** (Eugene Allen[6], Eugene Allen[5], Georgia Lucille[4] Cooksey, George W.[3], Samuel[2], William[1]).
    He married 'unknown'.

    Children:
    44.   i. Elizabeth Nicole[8] Briggs.
          ii. Caleb Briggs.

Caleb and Bailey Briggs   *Bailey Faith Briggs*

      iii. Bailey Faith Briggs.

32. **Bobbi Jo[7] Briggs** (Eugene Allen[6], Eugene Allen[5], Georgia Lucille[4] Cooksey, George W.[3], Samuel[2], William[1]).
    She married (1) Tony Lee Wilson.

    Children:
          i. Ashley Reyna Marie[8] Wilson.
          ii. Joseph Allen Wilson.
          iii. Reyanna Ivy Bree Wilson.

Bobbi Jo (Briggs) Friscia and daughter

She married (2) John Joseph Friscia.

> Children:
> iv. Amanda Sheri Phylis Briggs-Friscia.
> v. Isabella Rose Friscia.

33. **Georgia Marie[7] Matheny** (Joyce Marie[6] Briggs, Eugene Allen[5], Georgia Lucille[4] Cooksey, George W.[3], Samuel[2], William[1]).
She married (1) Charles Bresaw.
She married (2) Cory Poplett.

Georgia Matheny

Cory Meador

Stefanie Meador

Fylycia Meader

Christopher Meader

> *Children:*
> i. Cory[8] Meador.
> ii. Fylycia Meador.
> iii. Stefanie Meador.
> iv. Christopher Meador.

She married (3) Michael Meador.

34. **Robert Eugene[7] Matheny** (Joyce Marie[6] Briggs, Eugene Allen[5], Georgia Lucille[4] Cooksey, George W.[3], Samuel[2], William[1]), was born September 13, 1970 in Illinois, and died October 22, 2016 in Muscatine, Iowa.[55] He was buried October 28, 2016 in Smithfield Cemetery, Knox County, Illinois.[56]

Robert Eugene Matheny, 46, of Muscatine, IA, formerly of Galesburg, died at 10 a.m. Saturday, October 22, 2016 in Muscatine.
Rob was born September 13, 1970 in Moline, the son of Joyce M. Briggs and Harley E. Matheny. He married Paula Kennedy on July 15, 1989 in Kahoka, MO. She survives. He is also survived by his mother, Joyce M. Cox-Wright of Galesburg; his father, Harley Matheny of Abingdon; two sons, Robert Matheny, Jr. of Muscatine, IA and Tristan Matheny of Norman, OK; one daughter, Jensen Matheny of Muscatine, IA; and one grandson, Alex. He is also survived by two brothers, Steven Matheny of Abingdon and Joshua Cox of Chicago; and one sister, Georgia Matheny of Eldridge, IA.
Rob worked for Pepsi, Co. He loved riding motorcycles and spending time with his family, especially his grandson, Alex. Rob also had an extensive movie collection and was an avid Star Trek fan.
Memorial services will be at 1 p.m. Friday, October 28, 2016 at Salvation Army Church, Galesburg. Envoy's Lisa and Tim Thorson will officiate. There will be no visitation. Burial of cremated remains will follow in Smithfield Cemetery, rural Cuba. Arrangements have been entrusted to Watson-Thomas Funeral Home and Crematory, Galesburg. Memorials may be made to the family.

Robert Eugene Matheny

He married Paula Kennedy, July 15, 1989 in Kahoka, Missouri.

> *Children:*
> i. Robert[8] Matheny, Jr..
> ii. Jenna Matheny.
> iii. Tristen Matheny.

Steve and Sandy (Ellis) Matheny   *Cassandra Matheny*   *Samantha Matheny and family*   *Colten Matheny*

35. **Steven Lee[7] Matheny** (Joyce Marie[6] Briggs, Eugene Allen[5], Georgia Lucille[4] Cooksey, George W.[3], Samuel[2], William[1]).
    He married (1) Jennie Wall.

> *Children:*
> i. Samantha[8] Matheny.
> ii. Cassandra Matheny.
> iii. Colten Matheny.

He married (2) Sandra Ellis.

36. **Larue James[7] Meehan II** (Beverly Ann[6] Briggs, Eugene Allen[5], Georgia Lucille[4] Cooksey, George W.[3], Samuel[2], William[1]), was born April 1974 in Illinois.

Larue II, Alexis and Larue III

He married Shae Marie Webb, who was born September 1977.

> *Children:*
> i.   Alexis Nichole Ann[8] Meehan.
> ii. Larue James Meehan III.

37. **Wanita[7] Meehan** (Beverly Ann[6] Briggs, Eugene Allen[5], Georgia Lucille[4] Cooksey, George W.[3], Samuel[2], William[1]).

Wanita (Meehan) Stockton

Curstin Beverly Meehan

She had a relationship with 'unknown'.

> *Children:*
> i.   Curstin Beverly[8] Meehan.

She married (2) John Stockton.
She is engaged to (3) Marcus Almaguer.

> *Children:*
> ii. Marcus Wayne Almaguer.

38. **Patrick[7] Meehan** (Beverly Ann[6] Briggs, Eugene Allen[5], Georgia Lucille[4] Cooksey, George W.[3], Samuel[2], William[1]).

Patrick and Natalie (Reda) Meehan

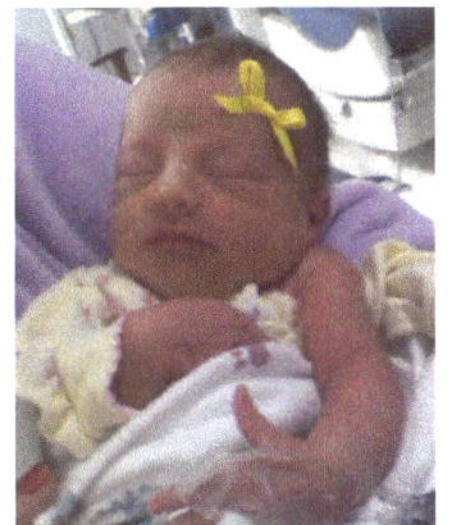
Noelle Jacqueline Meehan

He married Natalie Reda.

> *Children:*
> i. Noelle Jacqueline[8] Meehan.

39. **Crystal[7] Meehan** (Beverly Ann[6] Briggs, Eugene Allen[5], Georgia Lucille[4] Cooksey, George W.[3], Samuel[2], William[1]).
She had a relationship with 'unknown'.

> *Children:*
> i. McKenzie[8] Nickerson.

She had a relationship with 'unknown'.

> *Children:*
> ii. Larue Nichols.
> iii. Delanee Nichols.

40. **Stefanie Marie[7] Thompson** (James Allen[6], Marion Maxine[5] Briggs, Georgia Lucille[4] Cooksey, George W.[3], Samuel[2], William[1]).
She had a relationship with 'unknown'.

> *Children:*
> i. Alexzandria[8] Sapp.
> ii. Ryan Sapp.

41. **Melanie[7] Thompson** (James Allen[6], Marion Maxine[5] Briggs, Georgia Lucille[4] Cooksey, George W.[3], Samuel[2], William[1]).
She had a relationship with 'unknown'.

Melanie Thompson Kilian

Chloe Parkes

Children:
i.   Chloe[8] Parkes.

She married (2) Zachary Killian.

42.   **Adam James "Thompson"[7] Swindell** (James Allen[6] Thompson, Marion Maxine[5] Briggs, Georgia Lucille[4] Cooksey, George W.[3], Samuel[2], William[1]).
He married Megan.

         Children:
         i.   Tylan[8] Swindell.

43.   **Shawn Dustin[7] Thompson** (Jerry D.[6], Darlene[5] Briggs, Georgia Lucille[4] Cooksey, George W.[3], Samuel[2], William[1]), was born June 24, 1981 in Galesburg, Knox County, Illinois, and died April 7, 2014 in Illinois, cremated April 2014.

Shawn Dustin Thompson

Shawn Dustin "Hank" Thompson, Galesburg Chapel 32, of Dahinda, formerly of East Galesburg, died Monday, April 7, 2014 from injuries sustained in a car accident.
Shawn was born June 24, 1981 in Galesburg, the son of Jerry D. and Mary E. (Lufkin) Thompson. He married Tonya Johnson on May 12, 2012 in Dahinda at Happy Hollow Lake.
Shawn is survived by his wife, Tonya Thompson and three daughters, Tristian Aldridge, Kenzie Thompson, and Khloe Thompson. He had several cousins he was very close to as well. He is also survived by his loving aunts and uncles, and his

grandfather, Rex Lufkin of East Galesburg. Shawn has one brother, Jeremy Thompson of East Galesburg. His mother, Mary (Lufkin) Thompson of East Galesburg also survives. He also leaves behind his beloved dog, Jasmine. He was preceded in death by his father, Jerry Thompson; his paternal grandparents, his maternal grandmother; and his cousin, Caleb Lufkin. Shawn graduated from Knoxville High School in 2001. He then started working for Hansen Lumber, where he still worked at the time of his death.

Shawn was a great husband, father, and friend to all who knew and met him. Shawn had many favorite hobbies like fishing, but his all time favorite was mushrooming. He was already looking for trees to look at. He and his mom went every year and usually found several pounds.

Shawn had a great friend, Jon Hootman, who was the one who set Shawn and Tonya up on their first date. Jon thought of Shawn as a brother.

Visitation will be 5 to 8 p.m. Friday, April 11, 2014 at Hinchliff-Pearson-West Galesburg Chapel. Funeral will be 2 p.m. Saturday at the chapel. Cremation will be accorded following the funeral. Memorials may be made to the family. Online condolences may be made at www.h-p-w.com.

He married Tonya Johnson, May 12, 2012 in Dahinda, Illinois.

> *Children:*
> i. Tristian[8] Thompson.
> *She married 'unknown' Aldridge.*
> ii. Kenzie Thompson.
> iii. Khloe Thompson.

Generation Eight

44. **Elizabeth Nicole[8] Briggs** (William "Billie"[7], Eugene Allen[6], Eugene Allen[5], Georgia Lucille[4] Cooksey, George W.[3], Samuel[2], William[1]).
She had a relationship with 'unknown'.

Elizabeth Nicole and Madison

Children:
i. Madison "Maddie"[9] Briggs.

INDEX OF NAMES

[1] *findagrave.com online cemetery listings.*
[2] *findagrave.com online cemetery listings.*
[3] *findagrave.com online cemetery listings.*
[4] *findagrave.com online cemetery listings.*
[5] *findagrave.com online cemetery listings.*
[6] *findagrave.com online cemetery listings.*
[7] *findagrave.com online cemetery listings.*
[8] *findagrave.com online cemetery listings.*
[9] *Marriage Certificate.*
[10] *Death Certificate.*
[11] *findagrave.com online cemetery listings.*
[12] *findagrave.com online cemetery listings.*
[13] *findagrave.com online cemetery listings.*
[14] *findagrave.com online cemetery listings.*
[15] *findagrave.com online cemetery listings.*
[16] *findagrave.com online cemetery listings.*
[17] *findagrave.com online cemetery listings.*
[18] *findagrave.com online cemetery listings.*
[19] *findagrave.com online cemetery listings.*
[20] *findagrave.com online cemetery listings.*
[21] *Obituary.*
[22] *Birth Certificate.*
[23] *Obituary.*
[24] *Obituary.*
[25] *Obituary.*
[26] *Obituary.*
[27] *Obituary.*
[28] *findagrave.com online cemetery listings.*
[29] *findagrave.com online cemetery listings.*
[30] *findagrave.com online cemetery listings.*
[31] *findagrave.com online cemetery listings.*
[32] *findagrave.com online cemetery listings.*
[33] *findagrave.com online cemetery listings.*
[34] *Birth Certificate.*
[35] *Death Certificate.*
[36] *Death Certificate.*
[37] *Marriage Certificate.*
[38] *Obituary.*
[39] *Death Certificate.*
[40] *Death Certificate.*
[41] *Death Certificate.*
[42] *Obituary.*
[43] *Obituary.*
[44] *Obituary.*
[45] *Obituary.*
[46] *findagrave.com online database of cemeteries.*
[47] *findagrave.com online cemetery listings.*
[48] *Marriage Certificate.*
[49] *people search* (White Pages Premium online)
[50] *Birth Certificate.*
[51] *findagrave.com online database of cemeteries.*
[52] *findagrave.com online database of cemeteries.*
[53] *findagrave.com online database of cemeteries.*
[54] *findagrave.com online database of cemeteries.*
[55] *Obituary.*
[56] *findagrave.com online database of cemeteries.*

BIRTHS

MARRIAGES

DEATHS

If you would like to correspond with me and find out more information on other branches of the family email me at insanelyhappy2@hotmail.com

www.ingramcontent.com/pod-product-compliance
Lightning Source LLC
Chambersburg PA
CBHW040048240726
48664CB00004B/1103